BUDDY SHORTY JIM PRECIOUS MAX CAJUN MISTY TARTAN JOSIE TOBY ABE HANNAH CONNOR WOODY JESSIE CALLIE TURBO PHOEBE DUNCAN BERNIE RAZZ TAFFY CUPID BEAU EDDIE K.D. SADIE SPOT GUIDO WILLIE MAE ORBIT RANDY RENO BUTTONS GIDGET WINNIE TOM TIGGER PUSSYCAT LEO FOXY SCAMP SCOOTER ZULU WHITMAN SCOOBY SMOKY WAGNER FRED YODA BLINKY RUDOLPH MOOKIE BLUE CRICKET BARNEY SASSY SUNSHINE REED BOOKER WHISKY KIRBY CHABLIS ZOE OZZIE NOLAN MAO SANDY MOOSE MUFFIN HENRY MCDUFF HEIDI CHARLIE BRANDY CASEY DOMINO DICKENS HANS & FRITZ AUTUMN DANDY GONZO GINGER LITTLE BIT BUFFY ANGEL BABE MISS KITTY ALBERT MICKEY BILLY BLACKIE CHAMP OSCAR ARROW GYPSY FRITO TINA RICKY CHICA EBONY HOBO BUBBLES BUCK FROSTY FLUFFY KEESHA RASCAL POKEY KELLY HONEY FRISKY MITZIE SMUDGE IGGIE FLOYD FLETCHER COOKIE SPARKY FITZGERALD COSMO BRITTANY HERBIE CORNCOB RUFF BUSTER CAESER PETER ROCKY CHASE RUBY JASPER JASON HOMER BUZZ SCOUT CHANCE BEAN REX CHAUNCEY TOPSY PRINCESS CHESTER ARCHIE BISCUIT CHIQUITA DUCHESS CURLY JORDY DOYLE DREYFUSS PUDGE THUMPER BISHOP ROLLO HARLEY HONEY BEAR BEN WISHBONE SIMBA BOUNCE SAL LUKE SONNY PICKLES TOMMY JOEY IVAN TRIPOD CHEDDAR CINNAMON OTIS ICHABOD SHELBY MOE SPORT MILO ROMAN MANGO NIP & TUCK BRODIE SODA LAMBCHOP BLAZE CHEYENNE SHASTA COMET BLACKBERRY PEGASUS DAISY MAE MOCHA MILAGRO SEA MONKEY HICKORY BUTTERSCOTCH PIPER BLACKBIRD PESO KERMIT CHUBBY BENNIE LOVEBUG TOPAZ PIGLET SPIKE MISTER KENYA CUDDLES WILBUR ARTHUR CHEWY GHOST CASSIDY DEXTER CYRUS MORRIS JO CHLOE TUCKER CHICO CACTUS PANSY BOOP SISSY MITZI DINGO CUSTER COLA TYLER HARRY RED ROSE ROSCOE SINBAD GAL & GUY T.C. FIRE MOJO CHARCOAL BIJOU SKIPPY ALFIE CALAMITY BOO LUNA COLORS BOSCO BLITZ CONFETTI AMOS GOLDIE KENO MOLLY CASHMERE ROGER SEBASTIAN ENCHILADA BUMBLE BEE FRASIER BART OPUS LUCKY JAKE RODNEY WALDO BLOSSOM HAM BUSBY BRUNO LADY SEAN CHUCKLES KIMBA ELVIS GORDY TROUT INDIGO ROY ELF ANDY COPPER MONTANA ACE PEZ TEDDY BASIL REMUS WIGGINS SNOWY RIPLEY SHERMAN DINO SQUEAK WALKER MINNIE PASTEL MYRTLE JAMAICA PURDY ARGUS MINERVA MUJER KIWI PATRICK BERT CARMEL GERTRUDE SEYMOUR BUELLAH BRIAR PATCHES JACOB OLSEN DIZZY TOFFEY TANGO INDY EDITH PERCY SEQUOIA URSULA FERN BLAKE BANDIT CODY JED COLBY OLIVIA JAGUAR SMOKEY BEAR HAPPY VAN GOGH ROMEO CORY WALTER LOLITA ROCKET CALVIN MONROE ROXY HUCKLEBERRY SCARLET ZACK NELSON CLEOPATRA SNOWBALL WILMA TINKERBELL GOMER OREO BLOTCH PUMPKIN DEAN COCO DANCER TIPPER DASH PUFF COWBOY DAIQUIRI ARNOLD EMBER CHECKERS ARTIE DIGGER SOPHIE ROUX JUSTIN PEANUT MAGRUDER WANDA BETTY CHOCOLATE DESI CARMEN FLIP RIZZO GABBY RAGS HANNIBAL FOG ZIPPY CLEO BUCKWHEAT SIMON GEM KING & KONG TRISTIN PING MICK BINGO DAFFODIL MORGAN TULE PAPRIKA SETH ROMA GEORGE JELLYBEAN FRECKLES RUFUS CHIP OLIVE OYLE & POPEYE CAPER STRIPES NAT DANDELION ROCCO BANJO CISCO GEORGIA JASMINE SAM RAVEN JULIUS SPOCK D.P. BUTTERCUP BRIE LAD MOPSY JEZEBEL MIDGET HARVEY OLLIE SNOOPY DAPHNE PEE WEE TRAVIS SAUCEY CEDAR MURRAY COLE DIESEL STORMY SOCKS JOCK DILLON IKE THOR VALENTINO BARNABY TOBIAS TABITHA PEAR ANDRÉ FELIX LICORICE EMMET JUDE SALLIE FLYNN CAGNEY LANCELOT MISHA BAGEL JACKSON BING HERCULES ISADORA DUFFY JAZZ RAISIN GOBLIN MOPPET MILLIE TWEED MADELINE POCO THELMA & LOUISE PRESTON ZORBA BOOM BOOM HALLIE OLIVER PETEY SPUD HEATHCLIFFE ELMO DANTE SILK CLEMENTINE FLY PACO CORKY PABLO SIRIUS CADBURY VINNIE ROYCE HOBIE SQUIGGLES SHAMUS FUDGE REBEL DAISY PENNY TONY BUTCH BRIDGET SNICKER CLARENCE TOES HECTOR SYLVAN MINX BOOTS WHISKERS SYLVESTER HERMIT SID FINNEGAN TOWSER DUKE KIMMIE WIZARD CHILI JACK & JILL CHEROKEE SQUIRT SPITFIRE PADDINGTON SHADOW POLO NOODLE BONO SALT & PEPPER SPICE SMITTY FESTER AUSTIN MARSHMALLOW SATIN PANDA SONIA PRETZEL DOOLITTLE ECHO MARIGOLD SHARIF QUINN MANDY AMIGO EDSEL PIPPIN RUDY BELLA SARGE TIKI RHUBARB PETALS ORPHAN ANDY THEO ZELDA DIJON WILLOW DUDLEY CLYDE BRUTUS BLACKJACK CHRISTOPHER IVORY ASTRO PETUNIA NEWBERT BOOMER CHOPIN MACK LASKA TEX & RITA GABE SCOTTY CINDERS KATO BENJI GRAY CAT PILGRIM NORMAN JUDD ODIN TOSCA MOUSE MONTE PEABODY HAWKEYE PEBBLES BISMARCK ZACHARY RUFFLES ABNER JEEP OPIE BEA GUPPY CRANBERRY GILLIGAN MOZART DUSTY ORVIS DUFF AVERY BULLWINKLE DABNEY TIBBY MCGOO RALPH FISH CRACKERS FIGARO GARFIELD DEWEY RUSTY PIERRE KOKO PIXIE SUSHI BROWNIE SPUTTER TESS PINKY OSA OTTO PINKY PICASSO SCHOTZI TIMBER NEMO SPIDER HOBBIT SHEBA CINDERELLA WINSTON THUNDER SKIPPER ZOOM TROUBLE RIGBY TOOTSIE LUCY DINK SQUIRMY ZERO SQUIRREL CASPER BIBI DINAH FLO BARON CASHEW GATO KRYSTAL CHAPS DARBY DOVE FALSTAFF POPCORN PUMA MOXIE MARBLES MITTENS LUCAS CALHOUN YUKON SUNDANCE HERO HOUDINI GRETCHEN GENIE VELVET GRASSHOPPER HUEY OTTER TIFFANY ALIBI SASHA SHILOH ROOKIE RADAR HOPE INDIA JAVA PIRATE FELICIA SPRITE AJAX SKITTLES TACO JONAS MAGIC JET TOAD CLOWN MARCO PUFFIN BUGSY MENSCH TINY TIM APOLLO CLANCY TILLIE POSEY SCHNAPPS POO-BAH PUNCH MERLIN HASHBROWN TIP SAFFRON GRACIE ZEST PUCK BAXTER ASPEN CHARM DRAKE LEFTY HOOK GOOSE ABBY JINX PASHA THEO GALAHAD GIGI GROVER SKYE PLUTO IGOR SNUGS GOOBER BLIX HIGGINS HUMPHREY GRETEL SAGE MING PEACHES CLIFFORD STANLEY BYRON PAL

Happy
Birthday
Marlene

Best Friends

SUMNER W. FOWLER

Looking at all the
beautiful faces in this book
will bring a smile to
your heart.

Cinnamon
+ Suzie

Sumner W. Fowler

Introduction by Elaine Sichel

Best Friends

Portraits of Rescued, Sheltered and Adopted Companion Animals

V&V *Voice & Vision Publishing* ~ *Sebastopol, California*

ISBN 0-9643033-6-1

LIBRARY OF CONGRESS CATALOGING-IN-PUBLICATION DATA:

Fowler, Sumner W., 1944-
    Best friends : portraits of rescued, sheltered, and adopted companion
animals / Sumner W. Fowler ; introduction by Elaine Sichel
        p.   cm.
    Includes bibliographical references.
    ISBN 0-9643033-6-1 (sc). — ISBN 0-9643033-9-6 (ltd. ed. hd.)
    1. Dogs—Pictorial works. 2. Cats—Pictorial works. 3. Pets—Pictorial
works. 4. Dogs—Quotations, maxims, etc. 5. Cats—Quotations, maxims, etc.
6. Pets—Quotations, maxims, etc. I. Title
SF430.F68 1997
636.088'7'0222—dc20   96-28886
                                                                CIP

Printed and bound in the United States of America
Dedication quote from Mary Sidney Herbert

Voice & Vision Publishing, 12005 Green Valley Road, Sebastopol, California 95472

TO

Gus

1983 to 1995

My fellow, my companion,
held most dear,
my soul, my other self.
My friend.

Contents

The fox said to the little prince: Men have forgotten this truth, but you must not forget it. You remain responsible, forever, for what you have tamed.

Antoine de saint-Exupery, *The Little Prince*

Introduction

ANIMALS GIVE US MUCH, AND ASK FOR LITTLE IN RETURN. Affection, companionship, a bond. However you define a "best friend," it's hard to argue that the gifts of devotion, loyalty, and attachment pet animals offer their human companions constitutes anything but a friendship of the highest caliber. Though we typically say we "own" an animal, the relationship is usually much richer than simply holding title to a belonging. As a nation we are passionate about our pets (and fascinated by celebrity pets such as Lassie, Morris, and Socks). We share our homes with some 600 million companion animals. We spend billions of dollars annually on supplies, toys, food, licensing, grooming, boarding and veterinary care. We celebrate our companion animals' birthdays, talk to them, give them endearing names, and, when the time comes, grieve over their passing. Caring for a pet is a satisfying and enriching experience, and a substantial number of us delight in making pet ownership a part of our lives. For many of us, pets are family.

Yet, as in any relationship, there are also failures. Many of us betray our friends. We sever the bond, or never quite develop it in the first place. We revert to treating animals like property to be cast off, disposed of, passed along. There are many manifestations of the breakdown: The Classified ads reading, *"Free, to good home— adult cat, puppies, bunny, dog, two dogs;"* children offering puppies from

9

a cardboard box in front of the grocery store; a sign posted at the veterinary clinic: SEVEN-YEAR-OLD CAT. NEEDS HOME. MOVING. Or, simply, and most sadly, the stray animal we notice roaming our neighborhood.

Fortunately, for more than one hundred-and-thirty years there has been an organization that has come to the rescue when people fail to meet their obligations in their relationship with an animal: *the animal shelter.* The dictionary defines "shelter" the following way:

> **shelter** *n.* **1. a.** Something that provides protection.
> **b.** A refuge; a haven. SYNONYMS: retreat, refuge, asylum, sanctuary.... Places affording protection as from danger, injury or attack.
>
> *American Heritage Dictionary,* Third Edition

Animal shelters are all these things and more. Those who founded the first animal shelters (known as humane societies and societies for the prevention of cruelty to animals, or SPCAs) in England and the United States in the mid-1800's, and the people who staff shelters today, are deeply committed to animals. Without hesitation, animal shelter workers confront and try to remedy the wide array of problems that result when people do not follow through in their commitment to a pet. Thousands of independently run humane societies, SPCAs and governmental animal control agencies nationwide provide refuge to millions of stray, abandoned, and abused animals annually. *Best Friends: Portraits of Rescued, Sheltered, and Adopted Companion Animals* honors the work of these organizations by bringing together the portraits and stories of just some of the many animals who have been helped. Each animal pictured in *Best Friends* represents thousands more who are sheltered yearly.

By no means do all homeless or abused pets end up in shelters, but those that do are lucky (modern shelters are not bleak or antiquated "pounds" staffed by heartless "dogcatchers," despite the picture that persists in the minds of some). For a pet, life on the streets or in an abusive home is full of perils. Shelters provide homeless and forsaken pets with refuge in the form of a dry, safe place to rest, food, fresh water, medical attention if they are sick or injured, and most importantly, tenderness. In time of crisis, a shelter is a lost or abandoned animal's best friend.

When one considers how many animals pass through a shelter, and multiplies that by the number of shelters across the country, it is easy to feel overwhelmed by the statistics. The urge *not* to think about the problem can be compelling (which may be why animal shelters and the issues they address do not tend to receive a great deal of public exposure or attention). It is difficult for those of us who love animals to be reminded that people let their animal friends down on such a large scale. *Best Friends: Portraits of Rescued, Sheltered and Adopted Companion Animals* provides an encouraging reminder that forsaken companion animals are *not* alone. Shelters nationwide provide animals in need with care, comfort, and a chance at a safe and secure future.

Anyone who has rescued or adopted a pet knows first-hand how well formerly betrayed animals respond when treated with kindness and love. Animal shelter staff and volunteers are no different. Kind words, reassuring gestures, attention and love are the key ingredients for successfully nurturing animals and restoring their spirit; they are also the guiding principles of humane animal sheltering.

Best Friends: Portraits of Rescued, Sheltered and Adopted Companion Animals brings together more than one hundred images by photographer Sumner W. Fowler, offering proof that given the opportunity and the encouragement, sheltered animals respond to compassion splendidly. Sumner has been using his camera to document animal shelters for twenty years, and his pictures offer a warm—and inspiring—testimonial to both the animals he portrays, and the humanitarians who have cared for them at shelters.

As you turn the pages of this book you will meet many friends. Some were sheltered at the time their pictures were taken; others are adopted pets. Some were sheltered for only a brief time; others received long-term foster care while recuperating from injuries or illness. You will see that a variety of animals end up in shelters. They range in age from the very young (an orphaned pup being bottle fed), to adolescents (the six month old bunny who outgrew Easter), and the mature (the wise and contemplative older white cat). To learn each animal's story, see Notes on the Portraits on page 115.

In addition to mixed breed animals, most shelters usually have a high percentage of purebreds in their care. Spending a large sum of money on an animal does not guarantee fidelity; exotic animals, expensive Persian, Himalayan, and Abyssinian cats, pedigreed Cocker Spaniels, Rottweilers, and other popular breeds are found in shelters; any animal that can be kept as a pet will, at some point, be found in a shelter. When a particular species or breed becomes especially fashionable or the subject of a craze, there is also a corresponding increase in their numbers at shelters. Waves of Ragdoll and Munchkin cats, pot-bellied pigs, and "Spuds MacKenzie" Bull Terriers arrived at animal shelters in large numbers when their popularity soared. The novelty wears off, the reality of caring for the animals proves too challenging, and owners no longer want to keep such pets. They end up in a shelter's care.

Also surprising is the variety of ways animals find their way to a shelter: Rescued from a storm drain by a humane officer; left in a shelter's night kennel with a scribbled note reading CAN'T KEEP. LOVES KIDS; brought to a shelter office with papers and vaccination

records carefully organized; awarded into the custody of a shelter when an owner is found guilty of mistreatment or neglect. Some animals come with no story, others with a short one, even more with a lengthy saga. Death, divorce, relocation, incarceration, new baby, can't afford. *Don't want.*

Whatever their lineage or ancestry or age, regardless of the reason they have come to a shelter, sheltered animals excel at love and devotion. They are among the most eager-to-please, faithful, devoted, and appreciative companion animals you will ever meet. Their status as a sheltered animal, is after all, a reflection of human failure, and is not their "fault."

Caring and finding homes for pets who might have had a tough past requires skill, dedication and patience. And adopting such animals takes work too. But what successful relationship doesn't? People ask if an animal that has been treated poorly *can* learn to trust again. *Best Friends: Portraits of Rescued, Sheltered, and Adopted Companion Animals* answers that question with a resounding *yes.* Turn the pages that follow and meet just a few of the miracles animal shelters perform: witness the trust, sincerity, and warmth reflected in the eyes of our best friends. And finally, think about how we can live up to the promise inherent in having domesticated pets so long ago; how we can truly be *their* best friends.

Elaine Sichel

Elaine Sichel
Sonoma, California

For information on adopting animals or helping animal shelters,
see *Organizations* and *Readings* at the end of this book.

The balm of life, a kind and faithful friend.

Mercy Otis Warren

16

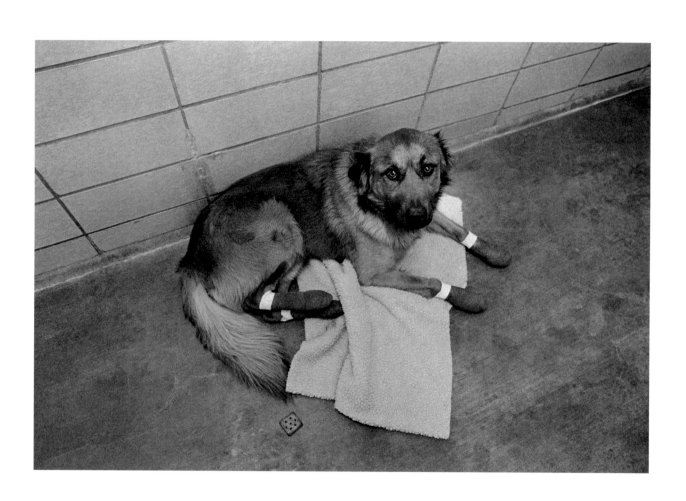

23

24

28

Animals are such agreeable friends;
they ask no questions, pass no criticisms.

George Eliot

34

44

49

53

54

The best mirror is an old friend.

George Herbert

59

64

73

88

94

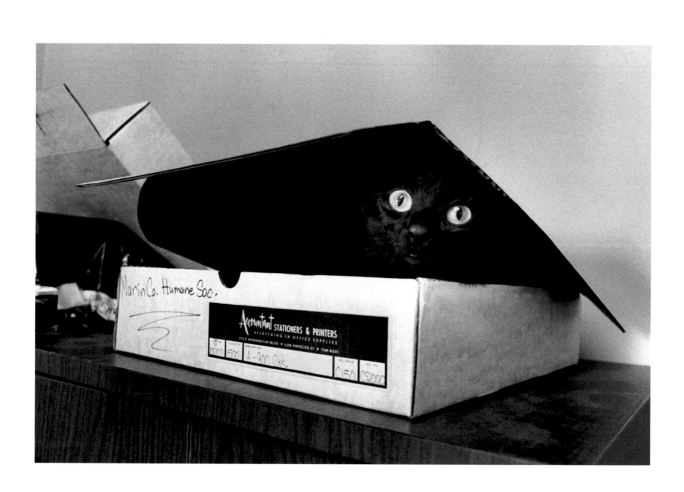

A faithful friend is a strong defense;
they that have found one have found a treasure.

Apocrypha

Each friend represents a world in us, a world possibly not born until they arrive; and it is only in this meeting that this new world is born.

Anaïs Nin

Notes on the Portraits

The following notes offer background on the animals featured in *Best Friends.* Where information is incomplete or omitted, details on the animal's case and fate could not be reliably confirmed. (Careful records are kept on sheltered animals, but their photographs are not a permanent part of their file.)

"Pet of the Week" animals were available for adoption at the time they were photographed. They are animals for whom homes have not been found; their pictures are run in advertisements promoting their availability.

❦

FRONT COVER

[Upper left] TOYON Found as a puppy in a dumpster, with cigarettes burns on his body. Rescued and adopted by 13-year-old girl (who went on to make a career in animal welfare). Lived to age 17. [Upper right] DOMINO Adopted. [Center] BUCKY Rat, adopted. [Lower left] ST. NICHOLAS [right] with friend. Animal control officers received call on abandoned, starving horse in pasture; property owner had never seen horse before. Gelding thoroughbred (20-plus years) rehabilitated and adopted.

REAR COVER

JAKE Cared for by an animal shelter after owner arrested; eventually surrendered to shelter. Put up for adoption; fate unknown.

INTERIOR

PAGE **2** GUS Left at a boarding kennel by owner, never picked up; kennel turned him over to shelter. Adopted. **5** GUS See note 2. **6** DOLLY Stray eight-week-old found on an ocean beach. Adopted. **8** WHISPER Member of surplus litter turned in to shelter. Adopted. **10** [top] ABERCROMBIE Abandoned semi-feral cat rescued by animal control officer. Adopted. **10** [bottom] NAMES UNKNOWN Purebred German Shepherd mother and son surrendered to shelter. Adopted. **11** COOPER Stray kitten, fostered, adopted. **12** CLOVER Purchased for $75 by good samaritan at horse auction; fostered and rehabilitated. Adopted. **13** GUS See note 2. **15** HERSHEY Pet of the Week. Adopted. **16** FRANK AND JESSE JAMES Stray orphaned kittens found in a paper bag outside a jewelry store. Dubbed "the outlaw kittens." Fostered and adopted. **17** ROBBIE AND JACKIE Adopted. **18** RUSTY Adopted. **19** SUGAR Pet of the Week. Adopted. **20** BRISA Adopted from a county shelter as a pup. With the facility at capacity, there was no room in the adoption ward. Spared from a scheduled euthanasia when her adopter dropped by shelter "just to look."

21 EMILY Member of surplus litter born on farm; rescued. **22** NIKE Improperly secured in an open pick-up truck, fell out and dragged on highway until tether broke. Samaritans found him, brought him to shelter, where he was treated. Injuries too severe for rehabilitation. Euthanized. **23** NAME UNKNOWN Adopted. **24** FRANK Pet of the Week. Adopted. **25** GUS See note 2. **26** COLORS An Australian Shepherd puppy surrendered with littermates. One of several litters surrendered by the same family. Adopted. **27** JINGLES Pet of the Week. Fate unknown. **28** SIMBA Transferred from one shelter (at full capacity) to another; adopted. During kitten season, May to November, shelters are deluged with "surplus" litters. **29** BEN Rescued after a misguided owner abandoned him in a shelter parking lot. Adopted. **30** TOYON See note for front cover. **32** DAVID Stray; victim of untreated and improperly healed broken leg. Adopted as shelter office resident and mascot. **33** BUDDY Surrendered to shelter by homeless person unable to care for him. Adopted. **34** MARLENE AND BETTE Fates unknown. **35** ST. NICHOLAS [right] See note for front cover. **36** SWEETIE One of four cats surrendered to a shelter by family of elderly woman. All were badly matted (a hazard when long-haired cats are not groomed regularly), flea-infested, and unsocialized to people. Two were euthanized, and three, including Sweetie, put up for adoption. Sweetie available for adoption as *Best Friends* went to press. **37** SMUDGE Found as an orphaned stray, fostered, and adopted. **38** SAMUEL Purebred English Yellow Labrador, surrendered as a three-month-old by couple who had purchased him in England. Adopted. **39** WILLIE Four-month-old Pit Bull mix, found terrified in middle of traffic; fostered by humane officer. Adopted. **40** PEANUT Mare seized in cruelty case. Peanut born while her mother was in humane society's custody. Shelter won case. Adopted. **41** BEAR One of a litter of Golden Retriever puppies fostered by a shelter director; adopted.

42 FRANK AND JESSE JAMES See note 16. **43** NUTMEG AND LICORICE Stray kittens, adopted. **44** MOLLY When a study ends or a dog is no longer needed, U.C. San Francisco Medical School has an arrangement to turn over research animals to nearby humane societies for placement. Adopted. **45** DOMINO See note for front cover. **46** GUS See note 2. **47** PHIL Abandoned stray found in front of a church (and hid by rescuer in her coat during services). Adopted. **48-49** NAMES UNKNOWN All Pets of the Week. Fates unknown. **50** CANDY Adoption puppy. Fate unknown. **51** NAME UNKNOWN Photographed while up for adoption. Pet of the Week. Fate unknown. Stray dogs are reclaimed from shelters in high numbers, but few people whose cats are missing look for them at shelters. Unclaimed strays are evaluated for adoption based on age, health, and temperament, and availability of space.

52 CLARA Adopted. Shelters see not only large breed dogs but also small and toy dogs—many of whom are purebreds (like this

Chihuahua). **53** ARIZONA Surrendered by family when owner entered a nursing home. Adopted. **54-55** NAMES UNKNOWN Pets of the Week. Fates unknown. **56** CLORIS Surrendered by owners—not enough time for her after baby arrived; adopted. **57** BYRON Pet of the Week. Adopted. **59** LANCELOT stray; adopted. **60** JILLIAN Stray kitten found with two broken legs by a family dog in backyard. Brought to shelter, underwent surgery to repair fractures, placed in foster home for post-surgical rehabilitation. To be available for adoption. **61** LADY Pet of the Week. Adopted. **62** NAME UNKNOWN Pet of the Week. Adopted. **63** BRISA See note 20. **64-65** WHISPER See note 8. **66** TROY Photo taken to illustrate a story on pet food. Adopted. (The pup was only allowed to eat an amount equivalent to a regular meal). **67** OTTO Purebred German Shorthaired Pointer. One of many purebreds received by shelters. Adopted. **68** JETHRO Abandoned when tenants were evicted. Adopted. **69** ELIOT Pet of the Week. Adopted. **70** EMILY See note 21. **71** BLIZZARD One of eight puppies surrendered with their mother, a purebred German Shepherd. Fostered. Adopted. **72** [left to right] LARRY, CURLY AND MOE Adopted. **73** CLANCY [far right] with littermates. Clancy adopted at eight-weeks and returned two days later. Re-adopted. Fate of littermates unknown. Many people assume adult animals cannot bond to new owners, so they choose a puppy or kitten. The young animal requires far more attention and effort than the adopter anticipated, and is returned. **74** RILEY Six-month-old Golden Retriever turned in to shelter with littermate. Adopted. **75** KELI First certified canine field agent for humane society; assisted in livestock rescues, herded stray sheep. **76** CAL Left at a veterinary hospital for treatment, owner never returned; adopted. **77** TOBY Adopted. **78** NAMES UNKNOWN Litter of puppies being surrendered to humane society. **79** NAMES UNKNOWN Details on case unavailable. **80** LORETTA Abandoned after a house fire; rescued. Adopted. **81** LORETTA See note 80. **82** PEANUT See note 40. **83** NAME UNKNOWN Pet of the Week. Fate unknown. **84** NAME UNKNOWN Adopted. **85** OREO Oreo's mother, while pregnant with Oreo, was one of 150 dogs rescued during raid on animal collector. Collectors believe they provide proper care for their animals, but inbreeding, disease, dehydration, and starvation are rampant. Oreo was born in a foster home and adopted (as were littermates and mother). **86** BUCKY See note for front cover. **87** CHAMPAGNE Appeared as six-month old stray on the doorstep of an elderly woman's home, adopting her. Owner helped found her community's humane society in the 1920s, and is the recipient of a Lifetime Humanitarian Achievement Award. **88** DAISY MAE and brother brought to shelter by good samaritans who found the pups on their rural road; neighbors found six more puppies and hound-mix mother—and took them to a different shelter. Investigation revealed mom and eight pups were dumped out of a moving car. Fate of all but Daisy Mae—adopted—unknown.

89 SASSY One of eleven puppies seized from a pet store for neglect. From puppy mills, all had serious health problems. Rehabilitated and adopted. **90** [clockwise from top left] TYRONE, JONATHAN, JASMINE, JASPER, AND KATO orphaned foster kittens. Adopted. **91** NAMES UNKNOWN Terminating its breeding program, a university planned to euthanize its entire beagle colony. Animal rights activists notified a local humane society; they persuaded the school to turn over the 100-plus dogs. Pups pictured were adopted. **92** DUTCH One of a litter of nine Basset Hound/Golden Retriever mix puppies. Adopted. **93** COOPER See note 11. **94** BELLE Surrendered by family who kept her tied in backyard because she was "out of control." Adopted. Participates in therapy programs with the elderly and disabled. Has earned numerous obedience awards. **95** AFFE [leaning into a catnip mouse] rescued and adopted by a shelter volunteer after she was given away in front of grocery store, too young (five weeks) to be weaned. Lived to 17½. **96** RUBY Shelter-adoptee. Assisted in the care of many foster kitten litters that were cared for by her human family. **97** BILL Stray (already neutered). Found bald and infected with earmites. Rehabilitated, adopted. Visits hospitals and nursing homes. **99** NAMES UNKNOWN Baby bunny found at a laundromat with littermates, pictured with an animal foster parent. **100** JESSE Surplus Border Collie. With high energy levels and exercise requirements people often can't meet, herding breeds come to shelters in high numbers. Adopted. **101** LIL One of 13 surplus Black Labrador mix pups, adopted by a shelter supervisor. **102** JED Rescued, sheltered and fostered. Adopted. **103** CLANCY See note 73. **104** SPANKY Pet of the Week. Adopted. **105** NAME UNKNOWN Owner surrender; Pet of the Week; Fate unknown. Dobermans, due to their popularity, are one of several breeds that enter shelters in especially high numbers. **106** JAKE See note for rear cover. **107** BOOP Semi-feral, stray, and under-aged; bottle-fed. Adopted. **108** RIPLEY Four-month-old stray purebred Boxer. Seen wandering for a month after California's Loma Prieta earthquake, rescued. Ill from malnutrition, giardia, and intestinal complications. Rehabilitated, adopted. **109** NAME UNKNOWN Pet of the Week, adopted. **110** HANS adopted. **111** BELLE See note 94. **113** ROCKY Found orphaned. Bottle-fed by a foster parent. Adopted. **119** GUS See note 2. **122** Sumner W. Fowler and RITA, Border Collie mix, adopted by Sumner from a shelter after being abandoned in an apple orchard. **128** DOLLY See note 6.

TECHNICAL NOTE

All photographs (with one exception) were made with Pentax and Nikon 35 mm camera bodies using lenses with focal lengths ranging from 24 to 200 mm. All photos were made using available light with 400 ASA Kodak TRI-X film. The photograph on page 80 was made using a 2¼ inch Mamiya medium format camera and bounce flash.

About the Photographer

SUMNER W. FOWLER, born in Maine and raised in Michigan, began taking pictures with a borrowed camera as a teenager. Photography became a career immediately after high school when he began working as a professional photographer doing freelance assignments.

In 1970, as a staff photographer for *The Ypsilanti Press,* Sumner suggested to his editor that their newspaper run a "pet of the week" piece featuring a photograph and information about adoptable animals at the local animal shelter, the Humane Society of Huron Valley (the pet-of-the-week feature was among the first of its kind; shelters around the country now routinely employ them to boost adoptions).

During his weekly trips to the shelter to photograph the animals, he became friends with the shelter director and his interest in shelters and documenting their work grew. In 1979 he took a part-time job with the Humane Society, making repairs on their aging facility and lending his photography skills to record the shelter's work. Ready for a change in surroundings, but not vocation, Sumner moved to California in 1980, working first at the San Francisco Society for the Prevention of Cruelty to Animals, and then the Marin Humane Society, where he continues working today, providing his photography skills and overseeing maintenance and repairs on the shelter facilities.

Thanks to the bequest of noted humanitarian George Whittell, the Marin Humane Society was just embarking on construction of a humane education center when Sumner came on board. Realizing what a wonderful opportunity they had to utilize his talents and what a difference well-taken photos could make in capturing the work and goals of animal shelters, a darkroom was hastily incorporated into the blueprints for the George C. Whittell Humane Education Center.

In the seventeen years since, Sumner has combined portraiture and documentary photography to record every imaginable aspect of animal shelters and the bond between people and animals: children's groups learning about kindness, training academies for future humane officers, mock investigations, breaking cases such as rescues and raids, before-and-after photographs of cruelty cases, special events, shelter staff and volunteers caring for animals, special rehabilitation and foster care animals, and of course, the pet-of-the-week portraits that started it all.

In addition to amassing a huge archive of over 100,000 shelter images, he has also instructed humane field officers on how to take pictures during investigations and taught darkroom techniques so that others can use photography to tell the animal shelter story. His work has been published in three books: *Circles of Compassion, Animals as Teachers and Healers,* and *Choosing a Shelter Dog;* countless national magazines and professional newsletters; and has been used by such prominent organizations as The Humane Society of the United

States, the American Humane Association, and the National Animal Control Association.

It is obvious from his work that Sumner has not only technical mastery, but profound empathy and respect for his animal subjects. Anyone who has ever tried to photograph an animal knows how difficult it can be—imagine trying to snap a picture of an excited shelter animal who has probably never even seen the person on the other side of the lens before. Yet what comes across in these pictures are trusting dogs, patient cats, calm rabbits, and poised horses revealing their essential selves.

Not surprisingly, Sumner's favorite pictures are the ones that, "really illustrate they way I feel about an animal, and the way they feel about me. A successful picture is one that shows them as they want to be. When I capture the animal's essence, I feel I've succeeded." The hardest pictures to make are not those that present technical challenges like a light-colored animal in bright lighting or a black cat in a dim environment, but the cases involving cruelty. "You absolutely have to get the best pictures possible because the case will depend on it," he says, "so even though you have to remove yourself emotionally somewhat to get the picture, you're there precisely because you care deeply—and the pictures depend on that."

Best Friends: Portraits of Rescued, Sheltered and Adopted Companion Animals brings together more than one hundred images from Sumner's archives to tell the animal shelter story. A few of the pictures will give you pause; most will make you smile. All will give you a greater appreciation for companion animals and the humane shelters that care for those in need.

Dorothea Lange said, "the camera is an instrument that teaches people how to see without a camera." Chances are, even the most passionate animal lover will see new dimensions to their animal friends—and themselves—through the candid and revealing images of Sumner W. Fowler and his camera. And even those of us who think we know about animals—and their vitality, resilience, courage, honesty, vulnerability, and humor—will learn still more from these photographs.

Sumner W. Fowler will donate a portion of royalties from *Best Friends* to the Marin Humane Society in Novato, California.

❧ *Organizations* ❧

For more information on animal shelters and animal welfare, contact the following organizations
(❋ *indicates organizations with a particular focus on animal shelter issues*):

AMERICAN SOCIETY FOR THE PREVENTION OF CRUELTY TO ANIMALS ❋
424 East 92ND Street, New York, NY 10128
Annual membership includes subscription to *Animal Watch.*

DORIS DAY ANIMAL LEAGUE ❋
227 Massachusetts Avenue NE, Washington, D.C. 20002
Sponsors annual Spay Day USA in February. Free Action Pack available.

FUND FOR ANIMALS ❋
200 West 57TH, New York, NY 10019
Also: Pet Overpopulation & Spay/Neuter Issues Office, 808 Alamo Drive, #306, Vacaville, CA 95688.

HUMANE SOCIETY OF THE UNITED STATES ❋
2100 L Street NW , Washington, D.C. 20036
Publishes *Animal Sheltering,* a bi-monthly magazine. $8 per one-year subscription.
HSUS also offers a catalogue of humane publications.

INTERNATIONAL SOCIETY FOR ANIMAL RIGHTS (ISAR)
421 South State Street, Clarks Summit, PA, 18411
Sponsors the annual Homeless Animals Vigil in August, focusing attention on
pet overpopulation and the work of animal shelters.

NATIONAL ASSOCIATION FOR HUMANE AND ENVIRONMENTAL EDUCATION
PO Box 362, East Haddam, CT 06423
Offers educational and teacher support materials on pet overpopulation and responsible care.

SPAY USA ❋
14 Vanderventer Avenue, Port Washington, NY 11050
Nationwide network and free referral for local low cost spaying and neutering. 800/248-SPAY.

❧ *Readings* ❧

To learn more about adopting animals or to help animal shelters, the following books are available
(*❀ indicates readings specifically for or about animal shelters*):

Benjamin, Carol Lea, *The Chosen Puppy: How to Select and Raise a Great Puppy from An Animal Shelter* (New York: Howell Book House, 1990). $7.95 ❀

Benjamin, Carol Lea, *Second-Hand Dog: How to Turn Yours Into a First-Rate Pet* (New York: Howell Book House, 1988). $6.95 ❀

Branigan, Cynthia, *Adopting the Racing Greyhound* (New York: Howell Book House, 1992). $13

Christiansen, Bob, *Choosing a Shelter Dog: A Complete Guide to Help You Rescue and Rehome a Dog* (Carlsbad: Canine Learning Center, 1995). $9.95 ❀

Harriman, Marinell, *House Rabbit Handbook* (Alameda: Drollery Press, 1995). $8.95

The Humane Society of the United States, *52 Simple Things You Can Do to Help End Pet Overpopulation* (Washington: HSUS, 1993). $3.95

Jankowski, Connie, *Adopting Cats and Kittens* (New York: Howell Book House, 1993). $8 ❀

Progressive Animal Welfare Society, *Hands-On Handbook: Everything You Should Know to Make The World a Better Place for Dogs and Cats* (Lynwood: PAWS, 1995). $1 ❀

Rubinstein, Eliza and Shari Kalina, *The Adoption Option* (New York: Howell Book House, 1996). $12.95

Sichel, Elaine, ed., *Circles of Compassion: A Collection of Humane Words and Work* (Sebastopol: Voice & Vision Publishing, 1995). $12 ❀

Sturla, Kim, *Companion Animal Overpopulation Resource Guide* (Vacaville: The Fund for Animals, 1995). $10 (Also, "Do Dreams Come True?," a ten-page illustrated story about shelters and pet overpopulation for school-age children. Free)

To order any of these books, see information on the next page.

Animal shelters, whether municipally or privately run, need community support.
To learn how you can help, call your local shelter—look in the yellow pages under *Humane Society, SPCA* or *Animal Shelter,* or check the local government section under *Animals.*

❧ *Ordering Information* ❧

Readings listed on the previous page may be ordered from ShelterSource, a service of
Voice & Vision Publishing providing animal welfare resources to individuals and non-profit organizations.
Special discounts are available on books ordered for fundraising, education, or training purposes.
Please call or write for details.

SHELTERSOURCE / VOICE & VISION PUBLISHING
12005 Green Valley Road
Sebastopol, California 95472
707/823-1306

To place individual orders by mail for items listed in *Readings,* please send:
1) A list of titles desired and price
2) Shipping charges ($4 for the first book, $2 for each additional title),
and include 7.5% sales tax to orders shipped within California

For VISA or MasterCard orders, or to receive a catalogue, call
800/560-1753

Softbound copies of *Best Friends: Portraits of Rescued, Sheltered, and Adopted Companion Animals*
may also be ordered by calling the above number, or sending $29.95 (in California, $32.20).
There is no additional shipping charge on *Best Friends.*

Deluxe, specially bound and boxed limited edition hardcover copies of *Best Friends* are available.
Books are signed; custom inscriptions are available by request.
Limited edition copies are $75 and include a print from the book.
Contact Voice & Vision Publishing at 707/823-1306 for availability.

For more information on Sumner W. Fowler's photography or to purchase prints from this book,
send a stamped, self-addressed envelope to Voice & Vision Publishing.

Best Friends

Project Concept & Editing by
Elaine Sichel, Sonoma, California

Design by
Troy Scott Parker
Cimarron Design, Boulder, Colorado

Composed in
Monotype Centaur

Printed on
100 pound Celesta Dull
10 percent post-consumer recycled content

Duotone separations and printing by
Gardner Lithograph, Buena Park, California

Binding by
Roswell Book Binding, Phoenix, Arizona

The 750 names at the front of this book represent
the number of new animals that come into the care
of animal shelters in the United States every five minutes.

VOICE & VISION
PUBLISHING

Voice & Vision Publishing was founded in 1993.
Its mission is to foster greater awareness and
compassion by bringing to print and a wider
audience the words and images of those
working on behalf of animals.

A portion of the proceeds from all projects are
donated to animal welfare and care organizations.